WORK
BOOK

ALSO BY STEVEN HEIGHTON

FICTION

Flight Paths of the Emperor
On earth as it is
The Shadow Boxer
Afterlands
Every Lost Country

POETRY

Stalin's Carnival
Foreign Ghosts
The Ecstasy of Skeptics
The Address Book
Patient Frame

ESSAYS

The Admen Move on Lhasa

ANTHOLOGIES

A Discord of Flags: Canadian Poets Write About the Persian
    Gulf War (with Peter Ormshaw & Michael Redhill)
Musings: An Anthology of Greek-Canadian Literature
    (with main editor Tess Fragoulis, & Helen Tsiriotakis)

CHAPBOOKS/LETTERPRESS

Paper Lanterns: 25 Postcards from Asia
The Stages of J. Gordon Whitehead

WORK
BOOK

memos &
dispatches
on writing

STEVEN HEIGHTON

MISFIT

ECW Press

Published by ECW Press
2120 Queen Street East, Suite 200, Toronto, Ontario, Canada M4E 1E2
416-694-3348 / info@ecwpress.com

Library and Archives Canada Cataloguing in Publication

Heighton, Steven, 1961–
Workbook : memos & dispatches on writing / Steven Heighton.

ISBN 978-1-55022-937-0
ALSO ISSUED AS: 978-1-77090-098-1 (PDF); 978-1-77090-097-4 (EPUB)

1. Heighton, Steven, 1961-. 2. Creation (Literary, artistic, etc.).
3. Authorship. I. Title.

PS8565.E451Z468 2011   C813'.54   C2011-902917-0

Editor for the press: Michael Holmes / a misFit book
Cover and text design: Tania Craan
Cover photo: Mary Huggard
Typesetting: Mary Bowness
Printing: Coach House Printing   3   4   5

The publication of *Workbook* has been generously supported by the Canada
Council for the Arts which last year invested $20.1 million in writing and publishing
throughout Canada, and by the Ontario Arts Council, an agency of the Government
of Ontario. We also acknowledge the financial support of the Government of Canada
through the Canada Book Fund for our publishing activities, and the contribution of
the Government of Ontario through the Ontario Book Publishing Tax Credit. The
marketing of this book was made possible with the support of the Ontario Media
Development Corporation.

PRINTED AND BOUND IN CANADA

How full of trifles everything is! It is only one's thoughts that fill a room with something more than furniture.

—Wallace Stevens

Any memo is both a *memento mori* and a love note to the world in its wondrous variety and profusion.

—Stamatis Smyrlis

Denn meine Heimat ist das, was ich schreibe.

—"So my homeland is what I write": unattributed aphorism from a German scholarly magazine, circa 1994

CONTENTS

W. B. Yeats believed that we turn our arguments with the world into essays, our arguments with ourselves into poetry. But is his idea—for all its neat symmetry, its epigrammatic authority—true of all writers who work in both forms? Giving the question some thought, I realized my own arguments with the world, and with myself, are more likely to gel into a form that's neither essay nor poetry.

Before I settle on a name for the form, let me explain why I use it. The brevity I can't seem to force on my fiction (I'd love to write four page stories, or 150-page novels) or even on my poems (I admire the haiku, but my natural leanings launch me onward for another ten, twenty, fifty lines), I bring automatically to these inner "arguments," which take the form of short, tight paragraphs, epigrams, memos.

Why not regular essays? Maybe because I sense that the full cosmos is clamouring to get into any essay a writer begins. To me, every direct statement about the world seems laughably incomplete—seems to imply and require its contradiction—seems to dictate, "Now tell the other side." Which I feel obliged to do. Which then mandates counter-contradictions and qualifications and so on, in a sort of Hegelian chain-reaction: thesis, antithesis, synthesis, leading to another thesis, etc. I grow impatient with the enterprise and yet the alternative would seem to be mendacity through omission, which is akin to propaganda. So I stick to a form that bluntly admits to its own limitation and partiality and makes a virtue of both traits—a form that lodges no claim to encyclopedic completeness, balance, or conclusive truth. At times, this form (I'm going to call it the memo) is a hybrid of the epigram and the précis, or of the aphorism and the abstract, the maxim and the debater's initial be-it-resolved. At other times it's a meditation in the Marcus Aurelian sense, a dispatch-to-self that hopes to address other selves—readers—as well. Even the two "essays" that frame this book exemplify the form, having accreted, coral reef wise, out of a group of impressionistic paragraphs and sentences, each one whole in itself and yet fragmentary: intended provocations, prods to further thought, dispute, and assertion.

S.H., Kingston, December 2010

I

GIVEN TO INSPIRATION

I am not bored at the moment, though it might be better
if I were. Boredom might mean I was lagging and loafing
my way slowly toward a fresh jag of creative work, creative
excitement—a poem, a story, the opening lines of a novel,
lines that might lead anywhere, into the expectant offing, off
the edge of the storyboard into a sandbox as vast as the Sahara.
(I chose writing because I saw no reason that adults should
ever cease to play.) Instead I'm expending another day as a
compliant, efficient functionary—earnest secretary to my own
little career. (If you'll excuse me, another email just blipped into
view. I'm going to have to click and skim over, so I can glean
that small, fleeting fix of satisfaction that comes from purging
the inbox. A sense of accomplishment!—the ensuing narcotic
calm!—that deeply licit, Lutheran drug our time-ridden culture
starts pushing on us in kindergarten, or even sooner.)

I'm afraid that boredom, at least of a certain kind, may be disappearing from the world. And this potential truancy has me worried, partly for the sake of my daughter and her generation, but also—how unsurprising—for myself. Myself and other writers. I mean, the minute I get bored now I check my email. There's often something new there—maybe something rewarding, a note from a friend, some news from my publisher. And if there's nothing there, there's the internet. For almost all of my writer friends it's the same: like me, they constantly, casually lateralize into the digital realm. Some of them also have cable TV (I don't), so if email, YouTube and other web excursions fail to gratify, they can surf a tsunami of channels. Or else play video games. Whatever. The issue here is screen media. The issue is that staring into space—in that musing, semi-bored state that can precede or help produce creative activity—is impossible when you keep interposing a screen between your seeing mind and the space beyond. The idea is to stare at *nothing*—to let nothingness permeate your field of vision, so the externally unstimulated mind revs down, begins to brood and muse and dream.

What a live screen presents is the opposite of nothing. The info and interactivity it proffers can be vital, instructive, entertaining, usefully subversive and other good things, but they also keep the mind in a state of hyperstimulation. All the neurological and anecdotal evidence backs up this claim.

The twenty-first century brain may be verging on the neural equivalent of adrenal collapse.

Just as an hour of boredom—of being at loose ends and staring into space—can serve as precursor to a child's next spate of creative work/play ("work," I write, because a young child's profession is to play), so an adult's month of brooding can open into a year of purposeful creativity.

———

Boredom is the laboratory where new enthusiasms ready themselves, beakers and test tubes bubbling quietly over Bunsen flames no larger than pilot lights, spectral figures in lab coats moving among them, speaking in hushed voices. Not one of these figures has the bored dreamer's own face—the face the dreamer wears during the day.

———

Sign on the wall of a corporate poobah in a Heinrich Böll story—a man who has a treadmill installed under his desk so he can both exercise and generate power for his office while he signs forms, dictates, and answers the phone:

IT'S A CRIME TO SLEEP.

What he really means is that it's a crime to dream.

———

Boredom is a hibernation, or aestivation, a remission from conscious thought and mental din, a vacancy that starts to fill with microdreams that the dreamer never actually sees as she gazes into space and the dreams elapse on a deeper level, the way unseen fish—not those splashy gold koi on the surface, auditioning, greedy and garish—move in the depths of a pool on which small, suggestive ripples now and then flex: impulses rising to the waking mind in the form of insights, structures, germinal phrases, or *mots justes*.

———

I suspect Emily Dickinson was often bored. Bored and staring. And out of her boredom, lines erupted, openings like "My life had stood—a loaded gun" and "Safe in their alabaster chambers" and "Exaltation is the going / Of an inland soul to sea" . . . Lines that poke holes in the tenuous facade between our public being and the world's true, ecstatic reality. Or say instead that after boredom had done its work, her dreaming mind—the nightmind—could reach through the wall into that richer place and grasp new thoughts in the form of those lines. The daymind, the wakeful will, always on the make, as conscious and calculating as a grifter, is too busy and *practical* to receive weird, metamorphic couplets like the one uttered by Dickinson's dead speaker who "died for Beauty": "Until the Moss had reached our lips— / And covered up—our names—"

———

When you're musing with the nightmind you *have* no name, no needy ego. You're an anonymous stenographer transcribing words from some higher or deeper self.

———

Boredom, yes, as in those moments when the eyes stare without itinerary—when the brain's hard drive revolves at low rpm, uncoupled from regimen, responsibility, the whole Logistical Life that *becomes* one's life in the middle years, what Hinduism calls the Householder Phase, to do to do to do to do to do. But now alpha waves are lapping at the shore of the mind as you depart the secretarial for the sacramental realm.

———

Flannery O'Connor, ill with the lupus that would kill her, worked at her typewriter for two hours each morning, when her energy was at its least feeble, then spent the rest of the day in a rocking chair on the front porch of her house, doing nothing, she said, but staring.

———

Don't just do something, sit there.

———

Boredom, even of this potentially creative sort, can be experienced as distressing and oppressive partly because the ego, that notorious control freak, feels itself losing control and wants it back. Keep purging that inbox! Keep scratching items off the domestic roster! Advance your agenda. Improve yourself. Perfect and provide, provide, provide. At the end of the day you'll feel you've accomplished, achieved, earned the reward of rest, television, alcohol, sex, sleep, though of course it's a crime to sleep, to sleep too much, to dream and pay attention to dreams. And so the ego, which hates being forgotten, barges back into consciousness, urging you to do something *useful*.

———

(It's the Buddhist teacher and writer Thich Nhat Hahn who says instead, "Don't just do something, sit there." A small act of subversion in a society that has no use for stillness, silence, inward vision—that extols speed, productivity, the manic pursuit of things that by their nature can never be caught and retained.)

———

The ego is as out of place in the sacramental zone as a commercial PR rep would be in the workshop of a woman I know—a woman who hand-sews the bindings of the poetry books she prints on a linotype machine, simply out of a desire to make something beautiful, enduring, and good.

———

Finding the words—or receiving the words, let's say—is a matter of jumpstarting the quiet machinery of dreams while in a fully waking state. A feat more easily described than done.

———

Here's one thing I notice about the ideas that come out of daydream or nightdream: they work, they always work. They might not lead to *Hamlet*, but they work. As for the lines of poetry that come, they're *right*, sufficient unto themselves, in no need of editing. In fact, they seem pre-edited and polished—as if the relaxed mind has done the necessary work and then, when the moment is ripe, has issued the lines to the dreamer like a *fait accompli*. "I know I am in a dark place because I / cannot swallow, & the wasps / are weaving hives / into the dead eyes / of the streetlamps." These lines of my own are not great, but they are poetry, possessing poetry's surprise and bizarre aptness and rhythmic/acoustical unity. I'll wager that most people who read them will see that they're nightwork, not daywork, and that editing them would risk introducing foreign material—the material of the daytime will—to lines that have a nocturnal, oneiric integrity. I have a number of lines and poems like this, but not nearly enough. I wish they'd arrive more often, such things, delivered by overnight courier, calling for no editorial surgery, no weeks or months of revision. I can't speak for all writers, but I speak for some of us when I say that we might do more if we could learn to try less, to relax the mind so as to render it vulnerable to inspiration.

The corollary: that the daymind is always running interference, censoring, editing, talking over the whisperings and vesperings of something deeper; that if we could sedate the surface chatter, the nightmind could issue its pre-edited offerings more often.

Some of those offerings might not only be poetry, but also key insights into how to change our lives.

Who was the Person from Porlock, anyway? You remember that obtrusive, anonymous figure who rapped, Coleridge tells us, on the door of the poet's residence while he was writing down lines that had come to him in a dream (probably laudanum-induced) from which he'd just awakened. "Kubla Khan." Some have suggested that the Person was simply Coleridge's invented excuse for not being able to bring the poem—which starts so famously, "In Xanadu did Kubla Khan / A stately pleasure-dome decree"—to an equally sublime conclusion.

I think the Person from Porlock is nothing but the daymind, the willful, meddling, obstructively conscious brain, returning to full wakefulness and seizing back control. It raps its officious fist on the door of the imagination and scatters the dusts of a dream that until then had been using the poet as a sort of Dictaphone.

In a wireless world, where the daymind is never allowed to doze off, digital stimulation and busyness amount to a rapping so chronic it grows inaudible, unnoticed.

———

Don't get me wrong. No one finishes a novel or even a book of poems without a hefty contribution from the daymind—specifically the will, overseen by the hungry ego. (Who could finish a 400-page novel without some ego hunger?) Inspiration and good lines can only take a writer so far. Still, in the end, writing that's all sweat and disciplined desire for achievement, a story lacking inner vision, a poem untouched by the nudgings of the nightmind, these have no deep resonance or aesthetic staying power. We have to remember how to invite and receive the words and insights we can't force to mind. We have to relearn how to muse, drowse and stare into blankness, adrift, dormant, even bored, especially now when our various screens are always present—firewalls raised between us and the reality of dreams.

II

MEMOS TO A YOUNGER SELF

To be relayed back through time to a writer starting out

1   Interest is never enough. If it doesn't haunt you, you'll
    never write it well. What haunts and obsesses you into
    writing may, with luck and labour, interest your readers.
    What merely interests you is sure to bore them.

2   Let failure be your workshop. See it for what it is: the
    world walking you through a tough but necessary
    semester, free of tuition.

3   Embrace oblivion. The sooner you quit fretting about your
    current status and the long shot of posterity, the sooner
    you'll write something that matters—while actually
    enjoying the effort, at least some of the time.

4   *Allow* yourself to enjoy it. Squash the temptation to
    accentuate, poeticize, or wallow in the difficulties of the

writing life, which are probably not much worse than the particular difficulties of other professions and trades. Take a tradesman's practical approach to your development: quietly apprentice yourself to language and the craft, then start filling up your toolbox, item by item, year by year.

5   Ignore Lord Byron, who wrote that "We of the craft are all crazy." He was largely right, of course; ignore him anyway. To romanticize the Writer as pursued by Furies, enthused by Muses, beset by demons—this is nothing but professional self-importance and self-pity. Writers have no monopoly on poverty, humiliation, self-doubt, or aggressive inner demons. Close your door and get on with it.

6   Momentum and enthusiasm can mean pretty much the same thing. When working on a longer project, ruthlessly guard and prolong the momentum.

7   In writing, as in life, "personality" is not character. Never try to be cute, to be winning, to audition for the reader.

8   Never try to be cool. A writer afraid of seeming square will never write anything truly cool. The purest definition of cool, after all, is not caring what people think.

9   Stand on the side of artifice—of worked and earned, elaborated form. Life gives us enough of life. We approach art for something different: more distilled, catalyzed, charged, and signifying.

10   Avoid earnestness and solemnity—those Upper Canadian
     birthrights—by cultivating a grown-up, crap-detecting
     irony. But don't always use it. Irony is effective only
     in balance with other modes. Much current discourse
     renders itself void and dead by the ceaseless, indiscriminate
     use of irony.

11   Don't be afraid to be earnest either, if the work demands
     it.   [see 8, above]

12   Stop straining to be "original" and, with luck and applied
     time, it just might happen.

13   You can only write authentically within the bounds of
     your own sensibility, but you can read and appreciate far
     beyond them. To develop a broad and generous vision,
     you've got to.

14   You don't "graduate" from poetry to short stories, or get
     promoted from stories to the novel. The only graduation
     is to better writing.

15   Careerist writers don't have friends, only allies. This is
     reason enough not to be careerist.

16   Careerist writers don't confront and relish challenges,
     they crash into obstacles, which they naturally resent and
     fear. This is reason enough not to be careerist.

17   There can be just one final arbiter of your work. Refuse to
     appoint anyone else as your judge and appraiser,
     executioner, potential *approver*—the one reader, fellow-
     writer, critic, editor, or publisher whose acceptance of
     your work will stand as an ultimate verification, a proof
     of arrival, relieving you of that impostor-feeling every
     artist knows (a feeling that simply shows your aesthetic
     conscience is still active). Resign yourself to the road,
     there's no arrival. There's no map either, come to think of
     it, but the sun is rising and the radio is on.

III
MEMOS TO A
WRITER A DECADE
DEEP IN THE WORK

1   Could anyone else have written this thing? If Yes,
start again.

2   Novelty is nothing more than a fresh combining.

3   If nothing is new under the sun, nothing is old either.
Time cycles back. The ode, the epithalamion, the epistolary
novel—all can be made fresh again in the right hands.

4   In the long run, curiosity and stamina trump talent.

5   What makes a period of intense creativity a joy: the way
it integrates an adult's productive powers with the playful
oblivion of a child.

6   Since your deepest preoccupations are the same in every
book you write, there may be a single, elusive title that
could be applied to all your books.

6b Trying to locate that title is to learn a great deal (maybe too much, in fact) about your writing and your mind.

7 Don't feel discouraged when you find yourself falling out with your earlier work. Dissatisfaction is the price of improvement.

8 Improvement is not just a matter of amassing technique. Coming through a hard time, transcending a grief or an addiction—these can clarify and deepen your vision while also improving your prose style by teaching you to focus on the significant and to exclude mere filigree.

9 Be wary of the "respectability" that comes with even modest success. The respectable lose their yen for transcendence and grow obsessed with fortressing a social position—two changes that contaminate the creative source-waters.

9b "Yen for transcendence": a will to surmount or at least confront one's inborn pettiness and laziness, to be worthy of life's wonder and better able to frame it in the right words, rightly arranged.

10 Never generalize. The world beyond the mind consists of nothing but exceptions.

11 Complicate it, complicate it. Truth is in the nuances.

12   Then simplify in the later drafts to drive the complexity underground, like a textual subconscious.

13   You want your work to have a teeming subconscious. In your early drafts, write everything that occurs to you, then cut ferociously. The materials you cut—the rich or jagged silences you create—are the textual subconscious.   [*see also* IV, 9c]

14   Or think of those editorial gaps as synapses that a good reader can bridge with sparks of insight, helping to turn a now-collaborative work into a brightly firing circuit of experience and understanding.

15   There's nothing less pleasant than editing yourself well; it means excising the superfluous, self-indulgent stuff that was—admit it—the most pleasing to write.

15b   Learn to savour the violent, vandal delights of X-ing out and hacking away those primping passages.

16   The problem with poeticized novels is that they aim for beauty without *truth*—the rawness of the real; sometimes the reek of the real—and beauty without truth is not beautiful but kitschy.   [*see also* VII, 19]

17   Solemn, earnest overwriting feels like overwriting. Overwriting leavened by humour (think *Lolita*, think *Sophie's Choice*) is a delight.   [*see also* IV, 8]

18 Good writing, to paraphrase Sir Ralph Richardson, is overwriting and getting away with it.

19 Good writing is underwriting and getting away with it.

20 The main virtue of overwriting is that nobody overwrites like anybody else. The surest way to sound generic and nondescript is to write too cautiously, to follow the rules at all times, to avoid affronting canons of taste. Writers writing ebulliently and extravagantly will sooner or later do it in their own way.

21 What makes the majority snicker now may be what makes the work last in the long run.

22 To listen to critics, pro or con, and take their words to heart is to subcontract your self-esteem to strangers.

23 Don't confuse story and plot. Story is narrative impelled by character, so it emerges from inside the material of your fiction. (As Herakleitos put it, character is fate— i.e., one's story in potential form). Plot is a dramatic contrivance deployed to entertain or to illustrate a theme. Plot is imposed on the material from the outside, and everything else in the work—character, detail, language, etc.—is subordinated to it.

24 The character's necessary freedom becomes the writer's fertile constraint.

25   We're defined as individuals not so much by salient
qualities as by contradictions, visible or concealed,
conscious or not. If you populate your fiction with
characters realized according to a staple trait—prickliness;
stuttering shyness; bucktoothed, bespectacled nerdiness—
you get one- or two-dimensional figures at best. To work
the feel of life onto the page, characterize via a person's
deeper contradictions.

26   Fiction writers may gamble when they create main
characters who are difficult to like, but they cheat when
they concoct characters who, unlike you and me, are
wholly sympathetic.

27   Better baffle a thousand dormant readers than insult
an alert one by being obvious.

28   The writing life, like life in general, has a sacramental and
a secretarial side. As years pass and debts and duties accrue,
the secretarial, clerical mode spreads like a lymphoma and
starts to squeeze life from the sacramental, creative side.

28b   Learn to be irresponsible when necessary, without guilt.
Let bills breed in unmarked drawers. Let the inbox throng
and fester. Lend yourself wholly to the momentum when
inspiration commands; take care of marginal things in
their own time.

28c   Habituation is the assassin of vitality.

29   It's utterly natural but slowly damaging to yearn for plaudits another writer has enjoyed; it's utterly natural and aesthetically healthy to read a good book and then set out to write one as good, or better.   [*see also* IX, page 68]

30   If, as the psychologist Stephen Kosslyn has said, the mind is what the brain does, the story or poem is what the words do.

30b   The dualism of our culture inclines us to see style and content—like body and mind, or body and soul—as separate. There's no separation. Art, like life, is a continuum of contiguities.   [*see also* VII, 9, 10]

31   Don't squander time and vitality keeping abreast of all possible trends in popular culture. Pop culture is a torrent of vogues, some deeply significant, some not. Keep an ear cocked, an eye prised, and mostly what you need of the culture will find its way to you.

32   Refuse to feel uneasy about the autonomous observer that more and more detaches from you and in times of crisis, grief, elation, humiliation etc. hovers to one side coolly jotting notes.

33   Cast a spell and the small flaws don't matter.

34   There comes a point when an hour of sketching objects from life or learning to play an instrument will make you

a better writer than another hour of writing or reading will.

35   Stare more.

36   Gape and loiter.

37   Every moment spent in full attention is a moment spent in eternity.

IV

ON READING: FIFTEEN MEMOS TO MYSELF

1 Reading great prose or poetry is like undergoing corrective laser surgery: it sears away the cataracts of habit.

2 On reading an excellent writer for the first time, two vying urges: to go and write, and to give up writing.

3 Always start by giving a book the benefit of the doubt, as if broaching the book of a known master. This is a reciprocal gift on your part, a generosity the writer has earned over the year, or years, of work it has taken to complete the thing. For the first twenty or thirty pages, even if it doesn't seem much good, stick with it and its author. It may be as unsuccessful as it looks, or it may be something new—something you have to learn to read.

4 When reading a book that doesn't seem much good, outbursts of scorn can be satisfying (much like sprees of self-pity, in fact), but simply harden the arteries of awareness.

5　When it comes to prose style, the line between dazzling and blinding is a fine one. The blinded reader has a right to wonder: why does the writer want me blinded? What is it she wants to hide?　　[*see also* VII, 8]

6　Don't choose what to read by means of book page burble, juried shortlists, or bestseller charts. Let time do the choosing for you.

7　Certain books situate themselves clearly on one side or other of the great watershed of sensibility, that temperamental divide said to separate romantics from ironists, the young and exuberant from the sharper and sager. These are the books that readers love or hate, with little or no middle ground: *Under the Volcano*, *On the Road*, *By Grand Central Station I Sat Down and Wept*; or, on the other hand, *Vile Bodies*, the books of Ronald Firbank, Guy Davenport, John Metcalf, Russell Smith, P. G. Wodehouse.

8　In his early books Cormac McCarthy, like William Styron, William Faulkner, and certain other writers of the American South, consistently overwrites but is saved from badness (by a long shot) through a certain *integrity of excess*—a total and knowing commitment to his style.　　[*see also* III, 17]

9　The novel of a writer working too fast, fluently, skimmingly, may have a facile readability and enjoy more initial success than a denser rendition of the same concept.

But the facile novel, spilling along a shallow horizontal axis, lacks the vertical resonance that gives the deeper book its staying power, and eventual success.

9b   Eventual success? But for every *Blood Meridian* how many other small masterpieces, initially neglected, still languish unread?

9c   *Vertical resonance* means a downward echoing, the potential for soundings into a textual subconscious, the swimmer's thrilling sense, when crossing a mountain lake, of unmeasured depths in the dark below the thermocline. [*see also* III, 12, 13]

10   Lazy readers are unwilling or unable to empathize with characters different from themselves. Seeking some kind of personal corroboration, they want to read about versions of themselves.

10b   Lazy readers are unable to love a work of fiction—or even admire it—if they don't love the protagonist.

10c   Every lazy reader is a kind of narcissist.

11   Essence of kitsch: the sanitization and lessening of the world through euphemism.

11b   Not just euphemistic words but also concepts, scenes, characters.

12 Sentimentality: not so much the triumph of treacle as
a failure of intensity. No subject is inherently sentimental.
A description of a child watching a sunset while cuddling
a puppy can steer shy of sentimental, given a sufficient
violence of observational intensity.

13 Reading the great poet Jack Gilbert's early, ungreat
justifications of his aesthetic: much of what he says is
generally true, but general truths are finally useless. Only
particular truth matters, in life as in writing.
[*see also* III, 10]

14 The great gaffe of middlebrow readers is to confound
literature and virtue, to seek and require conventional
worthiness in the literary tale or poem, in its characters,
its sentiments, its creator. But good writing doesn't
necessarily come from good people, concern itself with
good characters, or extol good behaviour. It comes from
and concerns people who are intensely alive.

14b Our definition of "good" is faulty, or too costively confined.

15 Sometimes, rereading passages of my earlier writing, I'm
surprised by the power or clarity of an insight and wonder
who I must have pinched it from. Occasionally, I remember.

V

ON CRITICISM

1 Good reviewers appreciate books on the level of
execution, aesthetic integrity, and achievement. Mediocre
reviewers judge books by the degree to which they
"identify with" or like the main characters. Bad reviewers
like only what they can imagine writing themselves
and lash out at anything they can't understand or which
threatens their vision.   [*see also* IV, 10]

2 The bad reviewer's art involves universalizing, in
authoritative, pseudo-objective language, a totally
subjective response to a book.

3 Complaint is not criticism.

4 Poets or fiction writers who publish criticism are always
striving to clear the ground for their own work.

5 Two ways for writers to be humiliated: writing something

true that nobody will accept, thus generating scorn, and writing something untrue, thus generating scorn.

5b Scorn, to a writer, whatever its cause, feels the same on a gut level.

6 Aggrieved writer-critics suffer from an understandable illusion: that if they can identify real flaws in the work of another writer, they must be inherently better, smarter, either in what they've written already or in what they will surely write someday.

6b But you can always criticize at a higher level than you can compose; you can always spot flaws in a classic novel that you could never hope to write yourself.

6c A main source of the habitual severity of certain young reviewers, especially when critiquing elders: the reviewers' quickly growing critical faculties converge with generational competitiveness, that natural parenticidal urge. Presenting the stereotypical Angry Young Male Critic.

7 There are few critics whose harshest opinions would not be tempered, or even reversed, in the wake of their own large-scale success.

7b Those few who can't be bought off by an invitation to join the frat—those for whom success is not a gag order—are the rare, great critics.

8   The writing life's cruellest irony: while failure can make
    you miserable, success won't make you happy.

9   The writing life's cruellest irony: the creation of good
    fiction and poetry requires a life lived with existentially
    open pores, while handling the public side of a career
    requires thick skin, a closed carapace.

10 The writing life's cruellest irony: publishing authors are
    mostly recovering wallflowers who now seek to earn,
    through their writing, respect, praise, prizes, admiration,
    love—things they believe, consciously or un-, will
    retroactively salve the formative rejections of their early
    years. In so seeking, they bring on their adult selves more
    rejection and vicious personal attacks than they could ever
    have imagined in grade nine gym.

11 The author's job is to try to produce a work that renders
    the editor redundant. The editor's job is to show that the
    author has failed to do it.

12 Postmodern academics' fixation on pop culture derives
    partly from young academics being in denial about
    what they are: slowly aging intellectuals in positions of
    authority and power. Because, in a neophiliac culture that
    fetishizes youth, to age is to fail; in an anti-intellectual
    climate, intellectuals are unhip; in a democratized culture,
    authority and power are considered (for good reason)
    suspect. Anything, anything, not to be uncool! To be

uncool is to be *old*, shuffling in bunny slippers toward your obit.

13 There's no such thing as a lesser genre, only lesser or better writing.

VI

ON POETRY

1   Poetry: the art of calling things by their true and secret names.

2   So that Mandelstam, in his famous sonnet "Leningrad," shows us that his childhood city answers in imagination to an older, effaced name, Petersburg.

3   Every time we use the wrong word, the world slips farther out of focus and reach.

4   The world may not need poets, but the earth does. The earth needs poets to substantiate it lyrically, redeem it from its current invisibility, make it again tangible to a human world that's decimating nature, or in flight from it, hiding inside hard drives, the web and other digital habitats.

5   Poetry demands a language not only stripped of cliché (that hoary guideline) but also stripped of commercial

valence. Contemporary discourse is shot through with the phrasing and attitudes of merchandizing. Slogans become idioms. Brand names become nouns or verbs. Commercial attitudes end up contaminating the culture and conscripting our behaviour and speech. Poetry is a precinct where such language can still be recognized as barbaric and ephemeral. Where only virgin, cold-pressed language has any motive power.

6 Why not retain art as a haven for those not looking to sell or be sold anything?

7 In order to do something useful with your art, do something useless.

8 Purpose of formal constraints, if you use them: not to show off, or to establish an allegiance with (supposedly reactionary) traditionalists or (supposedly avant-garde) Oulipians, but simply to compress and intensify your material.

9 Poetry is not the way we talk or even write off the cuff, but the way we always would talk, if we could, at significant moments.

9b Poetry as the ultimate condition that speech and writing aspire to.

10 In a song, music can act as an acoustical narcotic
incapacitating the prefrontal cortex, allowing lyrics to pass
straight into the heart of the brain—no delay, no skeptical
critique, no interpretation. A poem's verbal music can have
the same effect, allowing the reader to experience the
poet's argument or imagery more directly.

10b Poetry has this much in common with propaganda:
the musical elements of oratory, on the tongue of a skilled
demagogue, Taser the rational mind.

10c Patterns of alliteration and rhyme / punctuation / line
breaks / caesuras: a poem's *emotional notation*.

11 A poem's perfect ending: one that closes the poem and
at the same time blows it back open. Like a neat conceptual
synthesis that nevertheless spawns a new thesis, a thousand
new theses, antitheses, syntheses, in infinite recession. . . .

12 No mainstream in poetry. Everyone marginal. No fat cats,
no free riders, no lounging elite. And yet these puerile
gang wars. Experimental poets consider lyric poets
mainstream and call formalists retrograde, reactionary.
Lyric free-versers call both formalists and experimentalists
academic. The formalists too call lyric poets mainstream
and call the experimentalists . . . You're right, this is boring.
Just read the work and love whatever feels alive, whatever
jolts you into new frames of feeling and thought.

NEW FRAMES
OF FEELING:
ECLECTIC DISPATCHES

1 Truly integrated, enlightened souls may dispense wise advice, but they seldom write interesting fiction or poetry. They don't need to. The natural medium of the achieved spirit is silence.

1b The rest of us talk and write to find our way, and it's from the rest of us—with divided, conflicted selves—that good poetry and fiction might emerge.

2 When it comes to philosophical affiliation, in the long run it's better for a novelist to carry a Stoic's or a Buddhist's card than a Romantic's.

3 The work of talented writers can show a concentrated maturity of outlook—a wisdom, a compassion—not always apparent in the writers' lives. Writers, working well, cast a sort of spell on themselves. Years later they reread passages and say, How could I have known that then? I don't even know it now.

4   It's said that your unlived life will kill you. True, but not
    before it has killed or maimed others around you first.

5   A great source of energy in fiction: when a writer has
    a moral vision in mind but is also strongly drawn by
    its antithesis (as with Russell Smith, who has admitted
    enjoying the cultural shallowness he also critiques).

5b Without some such contradiction, you're a mere
    dogmatist or moralizer.

6   Morality in art is tectonic, not a matter of backhoes and
    bulldozers hacking didactically at the surface.

7   The essence of good prose is the same as the essence of
    poetry: a refusal to flow along with the default patterns
    of daily language. Good prose, subtly or not, defies
    conventional diction and phrasing to induce small,
    dishabituating shocks, jolting readers into new frames
    of feeling.

7b The virtue of good prose lies mainly in this
    dishabituation; it triggers conceptual stammers in the
    mind, momentarily rerouting hard-set neural circuits, even
    laying the ground for new ones.

8   The more worked and mannered the prose style, the
    more the writer risks distancing the reader from his
    characters. Hence the stylist's main challenge: to keep the

characters' heads above the roiling surface of the prose, visible and alive.   [*see also* IV, 5]

9   On poets who write fiction: while a literary novelist strives to get every sentence right, and a story writer struggles with every word, a poet is actually attentive at the level of the syllable—attentive to each syllable's length, stress, latent or overt music, onomatopoeic potential and so on. Over the course of a text, the meanings developed and/or stories conveyed are not separable from this interplay of syllables any more than the externals of a galaxy are independent of the microscopic dance of its atoms. Put simply, poets writing fiction build texts from the microlevel upwards.

9b   When it works, this molecular construction, this radical aptness of diction and sound, leads to writing that feels layered, textured, mysterious, complex, and symphonic. When it fails, the results feel fussy, showy, effortful, pretentious, or, worst of all, static—a bevy of pretty phrases standing around preening and admiring themselves.

9c   One way for the poet-writing-fiction to avoid this vain stasis is to spin a compelling story. Poetic writing that leads narratively nowhere may feel self-indulgently idle, but similar writing that relates a good story can add to the text's resonance and force. So lucky readers of Richard Hughes's *A High Wind in Jamaica* or Joyce Cary's *The Horse's Mouth* get to savour both a compelling yarn and a bravura verbal performance.

10 Reject the crudely categorical notion that the athletic and aesthetic are mutually exclusive—like jocks versus artsies at college. Maybe in France no one will take you seriously as an intellectual or a poet if you're also physical. Well, three cheers for the French. The fit Athenians who founded Western philosophy and drama—soldiers, athletes, daily walkers who did much of their thinking and composing on the hoof—would have seen the notion as irrational guff.

10b Like so much of our guff, it links back to Cartesian dualism, the theory that mind and body are separate.

11 All writers are driven by two starkly different impulses, in different proportions: first, a passion for literature; second, a desire for power in the writing world—power in the form of access to the attention of others, access to money, the respect of other writers, the help of other writers, etc. According to which impulse dominates, writers can be defined as either creators or careerists.

12 Observing another writer, suddenly a star: like most people who deserve fame, she is not cut out for it.

13 Failure and sadness are the great unveilers. Successful lives—much like secure and orderly lives—help insulate people from the brute truths of human existence: not only that death is always present and waiting with lessening patience, but that our fellow primates are animated by resentment, envy, and grievance as much as by love.

13b   Grief is the great muse.

14   Unforced emotions always find the right words. Forced emotions, forced words.

15   First, a deep idea generates a theory. The theory begets an institution. And for a long time after, the institution extrudes ever mushier secondary ideas and promotes this guano as proven truth.

16   An institution works along the lines of an unconscious organism—an amoeba, a bivalve, moved by primitive tropisms—inclined not toward truth but to power, survival.

17   Creative passions frozen into habit, inspired ideas into ideologies, noble causes into institutions, spiritual longings into religions, freed peoples into xenophobic nations. How to avert, or subvert, that narrative of decay? To be alive is to be molten, to flow, to course.

17b   Why does patriotism, after the last century and a half, *still* have a fairly good name? Be a partisan only of love.

18   When a poet is creatively on fire, each word seems to pick and ignite the next one, a smoking chain of *mots justes*. When a fiction writer is hot, every scene generates the next in organic succession. When an essayist is flying, every idea births its successor.

19 On keeping your aesthetic conscience clean: when writing a novel of today, in the realist mode, don't cheat. You have to engage with the particular banalities of our time, despite the risk that you'll get mired in the banality and fail to master it, like an epidemiologist fatally infected by the virus she's trying to decode. If you banish the banal—reality TV, advertising, slang—you'll have fibbed, played it safe for the sake of the prize juries, produced something fakely elevated, genteel, poeticized.   [*see also* III, 16]

20 An historical novel is easier to write than a contemporary one. While the novelist-of-the-contemporary struggles to sort culturally significant trends, details, and jargon from the irrelevant and the banal, historical novelists find that time has done the triage for them: the significant has survived, the trivial is gone.

21 As history becomes less sure of exactly what the dead were when alive, so fiction becomes freer to imagine.

22 War, as a crucible of human character, is irresistible to writers. It brings out the worst, and sometimes the best, in human nature.

23 Clerical hyperefficiency undermines creativity. It's as if inspiration can't sneak in between the cracks because, when you're manically accomplishing and crossing chores off a list, there are no cracks, no openings in your attention.   [*see also* III, 28]

24   All literature constitutes an existential wake-up call. The ringer can be set high or almost inaudibly low, but the call is there.

25   Viewed from a certain angle, life is all elegy. From another angle, all birth and christening. In fact, it's both, always and at the same time.

26   In art, as in life, you'll need to have a master, but it needn't be anyone but you.

27   Are we all running dry? Is the collective soul so depleted? Why this pandemic of unapologetic, *unattributed* filching from other folks' poems, stories, interviews, songs, even emails? Spare me the rationalizations about the free flow of information, and intertextuality as a postmodern condition. When it comes to plagiarism, these are vindications of laziness. Writing something original— influenced by the work of others without stealing from it—is just harder, heartbreaking labour, and *slow*. And the slowness may be the crucial point. Maybe our drive to hyperproductivity and achievement compels us to generate extra product constantly by using other writers' words as scaffolding, catalyst, or enriching import.

27b Or has the educated class's sense of planetary permission swelled to the point where it feels artists have no right to the work of their own hands and hearts? (The motto of that class: we're entitled to everything we have not yet destroyed.)

27c   Use others' words as scaffolding, catalyst, or enriching import so long as you give credit—or can cut those words in the final draft and the work still stands on its own.

28   A scattered, discontinuous life is the postmodern norm; most of us, raised in generic suburbia, come from nowhere; writers of this drifting cohort seek to root themselves in language.

28b   Each book is a room in the home that the rootless writer, the *deracinado*, seeks to build out of words, images, ideas, and narrative.

29   *Deracinados*—bred in suburbia, atopia, the generic North American milieu—might as well have been born in cyberspace and raised in the food court of an international airport. Or an Old Navy outlet. If they're writers, they have one authentic subject: rootlessness. They'll never have the Deep South of Flannery O'Connor, the working class New Jersey of Bruce Springsteen, the midcentury Souwesto of Alice Munro, the seething Victorian London of Dickens. Pretending to have a true place they know in a radical, intimate way can result only in frantic mimicry. Their life is a postmodern patchwork and they have no native soil. They can write only of their exile, create books that will be their one home.

29b   I am a *deracinado*.

30 Writers, like others, live in hope, only more so. It's natural, we all do it—but hope pitches us beyond the present, our one living possession. Hope means leaning into the future, anticipating a maybe instead of living an is.

31 As the lives of writers, along with everyone else, accelerate and fragment—as access to sacred as opposed to logistical time decreases—so the timeless slowly vanishes from our world.   [*see also* III, 28, 37]

31b The dreamtime of creative work is a turnstile to eternity.

VIII

A DEVIL'S DICTIONARY FOR WRITERS

If God is in the details, the Devil is in the definitions

AMBITIOUS: writer more successful than oneself

BUZZ: ignorant consensus of readers who have not yet read the book in question and for the most part never will

COMPLAINT: not actually a form of criticism, though often mistaken as such by reviewers

DEADLINE: date by which writer must perfect excuses for not delivering in time

FAILURE: phenomenon that allows writers to retain their friends

FRIENDSHIPS, OF YOUNG WRITERS: akin to the urgent, insecure alliances of small countries in times of war

GOOD FICTION: a collaborative confidence trick

GOSSIP: weapon in the ancient, unconscious war waged
by the group against the individual

HIGH INFANT MORTALITY: problem endemic to literary novels,
a low percentage of which survive their first two years

HUMOUR, WIT: for some reason a proof to many readers, and
critics, that a writer lacks aesthetic seriousness (hence, a failure
to recognize the seriousness of play)

LITERATURE: an education in complexity

MEMO: the musing of a harmless drudge

NEGATIVE CRITICISM: art of creating, out of an instinctive
hostility towards work that tests or spurns one's vision, a calm,
orderly argument

Thus, NEGATIVE CRITIC: writer in the business of disguising a
club-wielding caveman in civilized tweed

PROMISING YOUNG WRITER: middle-aged writer whose work
is finally gaining notice

PROMISING YOUNGER WRITER: late middle-aged writer whose
work is finally etc.

ROYALTY: foreign celebrities who earn more in daily investment income than most writers earn in a lifetime

WRITER: someone trying to extend childhood—its exuberant creativity, its capacity for timeless absorption—all the way to death, thus bypassing adulthood altogether

WRITER'S WRITER: one who lives at or below the poverty line

IX

ON TRYING TO WEAR
AL'S SHIRTS

Adapted from a paper delivered in May 2006 at a University of
Ottawa symposium, "Al Purdy: The Ivory Thought." I did in fact
deliver it while wearing a loud blue polyester shirt
that had belonged to Al Purdy.

One afternoon sometime in 1983 or '84, Dr. Leslie Monkman
of the Queen's University English Department managed to
bring both Al Purdy and Earle Birney into our class for a
reading. I was in my early twenties, just beginning to write
poetry, and in awe of both poets. Birney, tall and cadaverous,
read first, in a croaky voice, ancient and wavering. He read for
about twenty minutes and clearly it taxed him. He had a heavy
cold. He seemed to grow smaller and more concave as the
reading went on. He left immediately afterward on the arm of a
beautiful young Asian woman who looked as though she could
have been a student in our class.

When Al Purdy got up for his turn and peered down at us,
the crown of his head almost grazed the bank of fluorescent

tubes on the ceiling, or so it seemed to us—or seems to me
now. In a big, barging voice he prefaced his reading by asking
what we had thought of Birney's performance. Nobody spoke.
Purdy's high, sunned forehead was stamped with a scowl
and his shaded glasses made it hard to decode his expression
or even to know exactly where he was looking. After some
moments of laden silence I put up my hand and offered that I'd
liked the reading, but had hoped Birney would also read from
"David," his celebrated long poem. Purdy stared at me with an
unamused grin. A few long moments more and he said, "Yeah,
sure, nice old man like that comes here to read, what else are
you going to say." He took the toothpick out of his mouth and
launched into a long reading, brilliant and riveting.

If I was surprised that Purdy would crack wise about a
fellow poet who'd just left the stage—in fact, an older poet,
and one who, I later learned, had influenced and encouraged
him—it was because I was naive then, maybe a bit wilfully,
about a natural and unavoidable aspect of the literary world:
the competition. Every poet wants to loom tall. Fiercely
competitive poets like Al Purdy aim to loom tallest.

———

How do we come to wear the shirts of mentor poets? Is it
a good thing, or bad? Is it a gesture of loyalty or a ghoulish
appropriation? Or is it neutral—utterly beside the point? I'm
going to talk here in an impressionistic, non-sequential way

about wearing the shirt of an admired older poet while trying to fill it out in my own manner.

———

I'm interested in how envy and the competitive urge can undermine the work of certain poets, while pushing others to new heights of achievement. Irving Layton wrote wonderful poems in the 1950s and '60s—his neglected masterpiece "Cemetery in August" is a case in point—but then became a celebrity and funnelled most of his immense vitality and talent into his persona instead of his prosody. Somehow Al Purdy was different. He could be refreshingly frank, both in person and on the page, about his egotism and competitiveness, yet it didn't make him lazy and vain. He got better through the '60s and '70s. He may have kept one eye on the competition, but he also kept a hand on the Muse—that principle of energy that clearly resents a lack of attention and turns away from all neglectful poets. Al, somehow, never stopped paying attention.

———

I met him and Eurithe Purdy a few years later, in the summer of 1988, at the famous A-frame in Ameliasburgh. He seemed if anything to have grown taller. Over the preceding years I'd gotten to know his poetry well, this process having begun with an essay I wrote about his Arctic poems soon after he and Earle Birney gave that reading at Queen's. Now Tom Marshall and

David Helwig had brought me and a couple of other young poets out to meet him. We sat in a circle of chairs on the deck in the sloping afternoon sunlight and we drank beer and talked. David and Al talked, mainly. Al had only a vague memory of his reading at Queen's and when I reminded him of what he'd said about Birney, he smiled wryly as if to suggest, "I don't remember saying it, but it sounds about right."

———

Recently I happened on a fact that at first I doubted: in the morning, when you get out of bed, you're almost an inch taller than you will be at nightfall. I supposed that if it were true, it must be owing to the nightly relaxation of the cushioning tissues around the vertebrae and joints, while the body is more or less free from gravity's tight-wound guy wires. So that you get up tall, but then, over the course of the day, gravity slowly compresses and slightly shrinks you. As if a day were a sort of re-enactment, or pre-capitulation, of a lifetime's trajectory: the life-impulse boosting you upward as far as it can, and then, after a point, gravity starting to work you back down to the ground you sprouted from years before. With a tape measure I marked out six feet on the inside of a doorway—whose shape and size, come to think of it, are pretty much the same as a coffin's—and got my daughter, standing on a chair, to measure me in the morning and then again after dinner. And it was true. I was an inch closer to the earth.

Martin Amis puts it this way in *The Information*, a novel about
a writer who is shrivelling on all fronts: "Gravity . . . wants you
down there, in the centre of the earth." To say it another way,
gravity wants you under the ground. Gravity is the principle that
resents our fleeting verticality—envies the passionate aberration
of our being. In fact, gravity seems to take our upright posture
personally. Maybe the horizontal hours of sleep are not just a pre-
enactment of our eventual state, but a sort of daily gravity tax.

In her novel *A Game to Play on the Tracks*, Lorna Jackson
observes of one of her characters that "Like most men, he is just
under six feet but claims to be six feet tall."

A scene from the early '90s, one of our by-now annual summer
visits to Al and Eurithe Purdy in Ameliasburgh. Al has taken me
into his windowless, clammy, mildewed writing shed. It's above
ground but feels like a root cellar. Still air, muffled sounds.
From one of the bookshelves he pulls a slim volume—his first
published book, *The Enchanted Echo*, from 1944. "Here, have a
look at this poem." Al has shown me *new* work before—and an
hour ago, in the house, he showed Tom Marshall and my wife,
Mary, and me a broadsheet that Irving Layton had just sent him
from Montreal, then watched us as we read it. You could feel
the concentrated, impatient attention behind his dark lenses. I
had mixed feelings about Layton's poem and said so, although

I told Al I did like the final image. He seemed irked by this imprudent diplomacy and said, "Aw, hell, I don't think it's any good at all!"

Now, out in Al's creative sanctum, I felt I was being tested again. An awkward moment. These were Al's first published poems. I'd heard he'd disowned them, more or less, but maybe he'd had a change of heart, or had always retained a private affection for the one poem he was now asking me to read. It was clumsily rhymed doggerel, a sort of Edwardian pastiche. I hadn't known Al long enough to be frank. "Well," I said softly, "I think there are some nice sounds in it, but I guess on the whole I prefer your more recent work." Something like that. Al snorted, grabbed the book away and bellowed, "DON'T BE SO GODDAMN MEALY-MOUTHED—IT'S A PIECE OF GODDAMN SHIT!"

————

Maybe that was the secret of Al's continual improvement. He wasn't just in competition with others, he vied with himself. Was hard on himself. I believe it was Jakov Lind who said that a good writer is somebody who hates himself and loves the world.

————

I never saw Earle Birney read again after that one time at Queen's. He died in the autumn of 1995, I heard, after climbing a tree and falling and breaking a leg, or arm, or hip, then going into a downward health spiral, as nonagenarians will after a bad break. Apparently he'd been trying to impress his young lover and companion. "My love is young & i am old / she'll need a new man soon. . . ."

A good story, but it turns out to be wrong. The fall from the tree happened some years before. All the same, the poet's late climb stands out as another assertion of verticality, a gesture of ascent, in defiance of the way time and gravity are hauling us steadily downward. The sort of defiance that male writers, especially, always seem determined to play out.

———

Evelyn Waugh, toward the end of his life, replying to a letter from an old friend who had, he felt, damned his latest novel with dim praise, complained about her "loathsome note" and accused her of spelling out what he already knew too well—that his "powers [were] failing."

———

Nobody fears death like an egotist. And nobody is better equipped than an egotist to write about that fear that each of us harbours to some degree.

———

Robert Kroetsch, in his novel *The Words of My Roaring*, suggests that a potent erection is, for a man, the supreme assertion of verticality, a graphic challenge to the homicidal gods, like a fist or the Finger shaken at the sky.

Stand tall.

———

To generalize is be an idiot, wrote Blake, but then he generalized too. So, for what it's worth: male writers are driven primarily by a fear and hatred of mortality, women writers by a deep awareness of it—an awareness that does involve fear, to be sure, but also a kind of creaturely acceptance of the inevitable.

———

I remember saying to Eurithe, shortly after Al's death, that I thought Al was a man who had always taken death very personally. And she said, "Yes, I think that's true." I will add that I think his life's work in poetry was a way of talking back to death, to time and gravity—the gradual attrition of the flesh. In fact, Al competed with death—not just with other poets, mentors, and himself. I sense that for him this vying with death was the ultimate competition. And the beautiful fuel of his poems.

———

Sometime in the early '90s, John Metcalf sent me a photocopy of a now-notorious comic poem, a piece very much in the spirit of Amis's *The Information*. This poem, by Clive James, begins "The book of my enemy has been remaindered / And I am pleased." It proceeds in that vein for another fifty-four lines. I thought it was hilarious and mailed a copy to Al. In his quick response he said that he found the poem in bad taste, unnecessarily crass and cruel. I'm still a bit surprised by his reaction; it must have had something to do with how the poem's journey to him had started at the desk of John Metcalf, a writer Al had quarrelled with on and off over the years. But I didn't think about it again for some time. Then, around 1996 or so, I got a typed letter from Al that included, among other things, a copy of that same masterpiece of exuberant envy. *Found this under a pile of papers on my desk*, Al wrote. *Don't know where it came from, but think it's pretty damn funny and thought you might get a kick out of it.*

———

Does wearing the shirt of an older poet, now dead, demonstrate a sort of filial loyalty, or is it a gesture akin to the bear hunter wearing the pelt of something he has outlived? The truth is, poets are not just competing with members of their own age-gang, they compete also with mentors and pupils. And Gore Vidal has spoken of the "instinctive human will to prevail." But I don't think that's the issue here. The mentor-apprentice relationship is competitive in the same way as a parent-child relationship.

The child wants to grow tall, to grow clear of the parent's epic shadow, while still being held, at times, in the parent's embrace. A part of the child instinctively wants to grow stronger than the parent, while another part fears the achievement of that aim. As Homer Simpson says, "I think the saddest day of my life was when I realized I could beat my dad at most things."

———

Al's best poems, I think, are unbeaten—or, as the saying goes, they *stand up*. Maybe I'm just making a case here for aesthetic emulation, since the competitive urge is dangerous to a poet's growth only when its object is status rather than achievement. And the two things are not the same. They rarely equate as they ought to. The media, for instance, will never care much about actual achievement—only about status and rank, hype and buzz, scandals and angles.

It's utterly natural but slowly damaging to yearn for plaudits another poet has enjoyed; on the other hand, it's utterly natural and aesthetically *healthy* to read a good poem and then set out to write one as good, or better. It was the second of those urges, I think, that most drove Al's writing.

———

Why wear the shirts of a mentor poet if one's goal is not to write poems like his? My own poetry is increasingly different from the work of this poet I've learned from. So? I wear this shirt because it was a sort of deathbed gift, much as Al's mentorship was a gift to me. So this shirt embodies the support and encouragement he gave. I wear this shirt because it's my connection to a mentor who understood that I not only loved his best work but also envied it, vied with it, took inspiration from the challenge of trying to stand equally tall. I wear this shirt because it's a reminder of all that can't be kept but must be passed on. And to be part of a tradition. And, to be sure, out of love.

And I always envied Al his shirts.

———

For the record, I'm still astonished that Al himself could ever have worn this shirt. He was a bigger man than I am, taller, broader, thicker-boned. How did he ever fit into it?

———

In 1997, in Kingston, I got to read with Al for the first and only time. I was opening up for him. The audience packed into the Sleepless Goat Café was there for him, of course, but an audience that size will straighten any performer's spine and the atmosphere in the room was thrilling, so I was stoked to go. In a photograph taken outside the café just after the event, in front of 350½ Princess, Al looks as tall, dominant, and self-contained as ever, but in a second, candid shot, taken soon afterward, he looks smaller, receding into himself now that the energizing gaze of the crowd has been withdrawn. He looks thinner than

I remember, and his short-sleeved, collared white shirt looks baggy, like the skin of somebody who has just lost a great deal of weight. I sense the fatigue in his posture and behind those big shaded glasses. He's almost eighty years old and has just read his poems for thirty-five minutes in a room sweltering with a dense crowd and its enthusiasms, its mobbish yearning to converge on celebrity.

———

In the spring of 2000 I saw him for the last time, dying at home in Sidney, B.C. Jay Ruzesky and I drove up from Victoria and sat at his bedside for a couple of hours, talking with him and at times just sitting there as we waited for him to wake from another short nap. At one point he tried to eat a piece of bread we brought him, but he couldn't manage. Some people may die in their boots, but no one really dies on his feet. And no eighty-two-year-old, horizontal for the last time, exhausted and unable to eat, rages at the dying of the light. That, after all, was a young poet's prescription—a heroization of the mechanics of dying. Or, as Al himself put it in his de-poeticizing way in "How a Dog Feels to Be Old": "[This is] as good a way / to leave as any / (Dylan notwithstanding)". So this poet who took death very personally appeared at the end to have made a grudging peace with it.

And what do you, the apprentice, feel now in watching the mentor leave? Along with the inevitable sense of loss, you suddenly feel much older, like a child watching a parent die.

You sense how promise is no longer enough and it's necessary for the real work to begin. You feel the truth of George Eliot's insight—that it's never too late to become the man you might have been. Death as the gift of a call to life. Seems the front-line trench, long occupied by elders, who stood between you and mortality and other apparent failures, has suddenly been vacated. You and your generation are going to have to fill it, as you'll have to fill, or try to fill, the shirts of those who came before.

ACKNOWLEDGEMENTS

As always, I thank family and close friends for their love and support. Specifically, I want to express gratitude to Michael Holmes for editing and publishing this book—and for suggesting I compile it in the first place. *Workbook* would not exist if not for his insistence, and persistence.

I'd like to acknowledge those publications where parts of *Workbook* first appeared or were reprinted: *Finding the Words* (McClelland & Stewart, 2011: my thanks to editor Jared Bland), *The Ivory Thought: Essays on Al Purdy* (University of Ottawa Press, 2008: thanks to editors Gerald Lynch, Shoshannah Ganz, and Josephene T. M. Kealey), *Little Eurekas* (by Robyn Sarah, Biblioasis, 2007), *The New Quarterly* (thanks especially to Kim Jernigan), *Geist*, the *National Post Afterword* (thanks to Mark Medley and Brad Frenette for inviting me to guest-edit the blog), and the *Globe and Mail*.

Emily Schultz's copy edit was thorough, perceptive, and—for me—relatively painless.

A note about the foreword. W.B. Yeats's actual words were, "We make of the quarrels with others, rhetoric, but of the quarrel with ourselves, poetry." It was Bronwen Wallace who first used the "arguments with the world" paraphrase in her Kingston *Whig Standard* column, "In Other Words." When Quarry Press published a posthumous collection of Wallace's columns and other prose in 1992, editor Joanne Page gave it the title *Arguments with the World*.

My bad-tempered rant about due accreditation (VII, 27, page 51) compels me to note that the phrase "a harmless drudge" (VIII, page 56) is Samuel Johnson's famous definition of "Lexicographer" in his *A Dictionary of the English Language*.

———

This book is for John Lavery (1949–2011), musician, linguist, writer.